B A X T E R ' S
Turkey Hunt

Jill Chowanes

PAGE PUBLISHING
Conneaut Lake, PA

First originally published by Page Publishing 2024

ISBN 979-8-89157-434-2 (pbk)
ISBN 979-8-89157-474-8 (digital)

Printed in the United States of America

On a blustery cold Thanksgiving Day, Baxter woke up hungry and alone in his house.

"I am hungry and lonely," said Baxter. "I am going out to find someone to share Thanksgiving with."

Baxter pulled on his cap, put on an orange hunting vest, and grabbed a huge net. He headed out into the forest to find a friend.

As he passed Farmer Daulton's field, he saw potatoes growing.

"Oh boy! Farmer Daulton won't mind if I borrow some for my Thanksgiving dinner," he said to himself.

He put them in his net.

Next Baxter walked past a cow in Farmer Meyer's pasture.

"Oh boy! Farmer Meyer won't mind if I borrow some milk for my Thanksgiving dinner," Baxter said to himself.

So he milked the cow and put a jug in his net.

Next, he came across Farmer Mickey's meadow. He saw corn growing in tall stalks.

"Oh boy! Farmer Mickey won't mind if I borrow some for my Thanksgiving dinner," he said.

So he picked up a couple of cobs and put them in his net.

Next, he came across Farmer Monty's land and saw pumpkins growing in the field.

"Oh boy! Farmer Monty won't mind if I borrow some for my Thanksgiving dinner," Baxter said.
So he picked up a tiny round sturdy pumpkin and put it in his net.

6

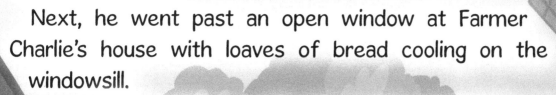

Next, he went past an open window at Farmer Charlie's house with loaves of bread cooling on the windowsill.

"Oh boy! Farmer Charlie won't mind if I borrow a loaf for my Thanksgiving dinner," he said to himself.

As he made his way into a clearing, he saw a beautiful colored turkey nibbling on some seeds by himself.

"Oh boy! He won't mind if I take him home for Thanksgiving dinner," he whispered.

He quietly snuck up on the big plump bird.

He looked down at his net, and it was full. "Oh boy! I have no room in my net for the turkey," he muttered.

He sadly walked back through the clearing and the pasture and the meadow.

When he got home, he emptied the net and made his Thanksgiving dinner with what he collected.

Then he had a brilliant idea.

He ran back to the clearing with his empty net.
As he got closer to the turkey with his net, he scooped him up and carried him back to his house.

When he let him out of the net, the turkey was shocked to see a plentiful dinner and the table decorated for Thanksgiving.

"Take a seat, turkey," said Baxter.

With a surprised look, the turkey sat down at the table.

NOVEMBER 2030

				1	2	3
4	5	6	7	8	9	10
11	12	13	14	15	16	17
18	19	20	21	22	23	24
25	26	27	28	29	30	31

They enjoyed a lovely dinner, and from then on each year, they ate Thanksgiving dinner together.

About the Author

Jill Chowanes is a four-time author. *Baxter's Turkey Hunt* is her fourth published book. She has been an elementary school teacher for twenty-five years in Pennsylvania. She lives with her husband, Joe, and her two dogs, Meyer and Baxter.

Printed in the USA
CPSIA information can be obtained
at www.ICGtesting.com
LVHW071244270924
792210LV00012B/157

9 798891 574342